The Essential Buyer's Guide

LAND ROVER
SERIES I, II & IIA

1948 to 197

T0169052

Your marque ex
Maurice Thurman

VELOCE PUBLISHING
THE PUBLISHER OF FINE AUTOMOTIVE BOOKS

The Essential Buyer's Guide Series

Alfa Romeo Alfasud (Metcalfe)
Alfa Romeo Alfetta: all saloon/sedan models 1972 to 1984 & coupé
models 1974 to 1987 (Metcalfe)
Alfa Romeo Giulia GT Coupé (Booker)
Alfa Romeo Giulia Spider (Booker)
Audi TT (Davies)
Audi TT Mk2 2006 to 2014 (Durnan)
Austin-Healey Big Healeys (Trummel)
BMW Boxer Twins (Henshaw)
BMW E30 3 Series 1981 to 1994 (Hosier)
BMW GS (Henshaw)
BMW X5 (Saunders)
BMW Z3 Roadster (Fishwick)
BMW Z4: E85 Roadster and E86 Coupé including M and Alpina 2003 to
2009 (Smitheram)
BSA 350, 441 & 500 Singles (Henshaw)
BSA 500 & 650 Twins (Henshaw)
BSA Bantam (Henshaw)
Choosing, Using & Maintaining Your Electric Bicycle (Henshaw)
Citroën 2CV (Paxton)
Citroën DS & ID (Heilig)
Cobra Replicas (Ayre)
Corvette C2 Sting Ray 1963-1967 (Falconer)
Datsun 240Z 1969 to 1973 (Newlyn)
DeLorean DMC-12 1981 to 1983 (Williams)
Ducati Bevel Twins (Falloon)
Ducati Desmodue Twins (Falloon)
Ducati Desmoquattro Twins – 851, 888, 916, 996, 998, ST4 1988 to 2004
(Falloon)
Fiat 500 & 600 (Bobbitt)
Ford Capri (Paxton)
Ford Escort Mk1 & Mk2 (Williamson)
Ford Focus RS/ST 1st Generation (Williamson)
Ford Model A – All Models 1927 to 1931 (Buckley)
Ford Model T – All models 1909 to 1927 (Barker)
Ford Mustang – First Generation 1964 to 1973 (Cook)
Ford Mustang – Fifth Generation (2005-2014) (Cook)
Ford RS Cosworth Sierra & Escort (Williamson)
Harley-Davidson Big Twins (Henshaw)
Hillman Imp (Morgan)
Hinckley Triumph triples & fours 750, 900, 955, 1000, 1050, 1200 – 1991-
2009 (Henshaw)
Honda CBR FireBlade (Henshaw)
Honda CBR600 Hurricane (Henshaw)
Honda SOHC Fours 1969-1984 (Henshaw)
Jaguar E-Type 3.8 & 4.2 litre (Crespin)
Jaguar E-type V12 5.3 litre (Crespin)
Jaguar Mark 1 & 2 (All models including Daimler 2.5-litre V8) 1955 to 1969
(Thorley)
Jaguar New XK 2005-2014 (Thorley)
Jaguar S-Type – 1999 to 2007 (Thorley)
Jaguar X-Type – 2001 to 2009 (Thorley)
Jaguar XJ-S (Crespin)
Jaguar XK 120, 140 & 150 (Thorley)
Jaguar XK8 & XKR (1996-2005) (Thorley)
Jaguar/Daimler XJ 1994-2003 (Crespin)
Jaguar/Daimler XJ40 (Crespin)
Jaguar/Daimler XJ6, XJ12 & Sovereign (Crespin)
Kawasaki Z1 & Z900 (Orritt)
Land Rover Discovery Series 1 (1989-1998) (Taylor)
Land Rover Discovery Series 2 (1998-2004) (Taylor)
Land Rover Series I, II & IIA (Thurman)
Land Rover Series III (Thurman)
Lotus Elan, S1 to Sprint and Plus 2 to Plus 2S 130/5 1962 to 1974 (Vale)
Lotus Europa, S1, S2, Twin-cam & Special 1966 to 1975 (Vale)
Lotus Seven replicas & Caterham 7: 1973-2013 (Hawkins)
Mazda MX-5 Miata (Mk1 1989-97 & Mk2 98-2001) (Crook)
Mazda RX-8 (Parish)
Mercedes-Benz 190: all 190 models (W201 series) 1982 to 1993 (Parish)
Mercedes-Benz 280-560SL & SLC (Bass)
Mercedes-Benz G-Wagen (Greene)

Mercedes-Benz Pagoda 230SL, 250SL & 280SL roadsters & coupés
(Bass)
Mercedes-Benz S-Class W126 Series (Zoporowski)
Mercedes-Benz S-Class Second Generation W116 Series (Parish)
Mercedes-Benz SL R129-series 1989 to 2001 (Parish)
Mercedes-Benz SLK (Bass)
Mercedes-Benz W123 (Parish)
Mercedes-Benz W124 – All models 1984-1997 (Zoporowski)
MG Midget & A-H Sprite (Horler)
MG TD, TF & TF1500 (Jones)
MGA 1955-1962 (Crosier)
MGB & MGB GT (Williams)
MGF & MG TF (Hawkins)
Mini (Paxton)
Morgan Plus 4 (Benfield)
Morris Minor & 1000 (Newell)
Moto Guzzi 2-valve big twins (Falloon)
New Mini (Collins)
Norton Commando (Henshaw)
Peugeot 205 GTI (Blackburn)
Piaggio Scooters – all modern two-stroke & four-stroke automatic models
1991 to 2016 (Willis)
Porsche 356 (Johnson)
Porsche 911 (964) (Streather)
Porsche 911 (991) (Streather)
Porsche 911 (993) (Streather)
Porsche 911 (996) (Streather)
Porsche 911 (997) – Model years 2004 to 2009 (Streather)
Porsche 911 (997) – Second generation models 2009 to 2012 (Streather)
Porsche 911 Carrera 3.2 (Streather)
Porsche 911SC (Streather)
Porsche 924 – All models 1976 to 1988 (Hodgkins)
Porsche 928 (Hemmings)
Porsche 930 Turbo & 911 (930) Turbo (Streather)
Porsche 944 (Higgins)
Porsche 981 Boxster & Cayman (Streather)
Porsche 986 Boxster (Streather)
Porsche 987 Boxster and Cayman 1st generation
(2005-2009) (Streather)
Porsche 987 Boxster and Cayman 2nd generation (2009-2012) (Streather)
Range Rover – First Generation models 1970 to 1996 (Taylor)
Range Rover – Second Generation 1994-2001 (Taylor)
Range Rover – Third Generation L322 (2002-2012) (Taylor)
Reliant Scimitar GTE (Payne)
Rolls-Royce Silver Shadow & Bentley T-Series (Bobbitt)
Rover 2000, 2200 & 3500 (Marrocco)
Royal Enfield Bullet (Henshaw)
Subaru Impreza (Hobbs)
Sunbeam Alpine (Barker)
Triumph 350 & 500 Twins (Henshaw)
Triumph Bonneville (Henshaw)
Triumph Herald & Vitesse (Ayre)
Triumph Spitfire and GT6 (Ayre)
Triumph Stag (Mort)
Triumph Thunderbird, Trophy & Tiger (Henshaw)
Triumph TR2 & TR3 - All models (including 3A & 3B) 1953 to 1962
(Conners)
Triumph TR4/4A & TR5/250 - All models 1961 to 1968 (Child & Battyll)
Triumph TR6 (Williams)
Triumph TR7 & TR8 (Williams)
Triumph Trident & BSA Rocket III (Rooke)
TVR Chimaera and Griffith (Kitchen)
TVR S-series (Kitchen)
Velocette 350 & 500 Singles 1946 to 1970 (Henshaw)
Vespa Scooters – Classic 2-stroke models 1960-2008 (Paxton)
Volkswagen Bus (Copping)
Volkswagen Transporter T4 (1990-2003) (Copping/Cservenka)
VW Golf GTI (Copping)
VW Beetle (Copping)
Volvo 700/900 Series (Beavis)
Volvo P1800/1800S, E & ES 1961 to 1973 (Murray)

www.veloce.co.uk

First published in April 2011, reprinted July 2016 and November 2019 by Veloce Publishing Limited, Veloce House, Parkway Farm Business Park, Middle Farm Way,
Poundbury, Dorchester, Dorset, DT1 3AR, England. Tel 01305 260068/Fax 01305 250479
e-mail info@veloce.co.uk/web www.veloce.co.uk or www.velocebooks.com.

ISBN: 978-1-787116-56-6 UPC: 6-36847-01656-2

British Library Cataloguing in Publication Data – A catalogue record for this book is available from the British Library. Typesetting, design and page make-up all by Veloce
Publishing Ltd on Apple Mac.
Printed and bound by CPI Group (UK) Ltd, Croydon, CR0 4YY.

Introduction & thanks
– the purpose of this book

This book provides a quick, step-by-step guide to selecting a Series I, II or IIA Land Rover that is appropriate for both your budget and your intended use.

Budgeting is important, so take care not to fall into the trap of setting out to buy the most expensive model you can afford, only to discover later that funds are not available to make desired modifications or repairs. There are many body and transmission parts that are interchangeable across several different models covered by this guide. Even some engines are interchangeable, too. You will need to decide, how authentic-to-year your budget allows your Land Rover to be.

A wide range of after-market accessories have been made available for Series Land Rovers over the years; as a result, no two vehicles are the same. Many of these accessories are referred to in this guide.

The high-shouldered doors are the most visibly characteristic feature of the Series I.

You can best check current UK market prices in the classified sections of the three main Land Rover magazines: *Land Rover Owner International*; *Land Rover Monthly* and *Classic Land Rover*. These magazines are available worldwide, but vehicle sales markets vary according to country – Series Land Rovers are significantly more expensive in the USA than in the UK, and similarly in other countries, where there is strong collector interest. The models are generally cheaper in developing countries, where you are likely to find that they have been locally modified.

Do not be concerned that a seller may consider you are wasting their time if you thoroughly examine the vehicle and then decide not to buy. You need to find the vehicle that is right for you. Do not expect to find it at the first attempt, and be prepared to travel long distances. Knowledge gained from reading this book should equip you with the most searching questions to ask over the phone or by email correspondence, limiting unproductive journeys as much as possible.

Buying from a reputable dealer will be more expensive, but then you get more guarantees of quality, and a degree of redress if something goes wrong. The private seller cannot offer you the same degree of security; this book provides you with the basis for a more confident purchase.

Detailed advice and technical data have been included throughout, so it can serve as a useful ongoing resource during vehicle ownership.

A variety of soft tops, hardtops, and Station Wagons are available across the range.

Over half a million vehicles come within the scope of this guide, with about 70 per cent of those being originally exported from the UK. So, if you search, you can expect to find a Series I, II or IIA Land Rover in almost any corner of the world; many are in sleep mode, however, awaiting a restoration project.

For the last two years of Series IIA production, the headlamps were mounted in the wings.

Thanks

I would like to thank the numerous members of The Land Rover Register (1948-53), The Land Rover Series I Club Ltd, and The Land Rover Series 2 Club. Each has provided me with much information over the years whilst publicly displaying its vehicles at various shows across the UK. Front cover image supplied by Roberto Hirth.

Contents

The Essential Buyer's Guide™ currency
At the time of publication a BG unit of currency "●" equals approximately
£1.00/US$1.22/Euro 1.11. Please adjust to suit current exchange rates
using Sterling as the base currency.

1 Is it the right vehicle for you?
– marriage guidance

Tall and short drivers
Seats are not adjustable. Drivers over 6ft (1.85m) have limited legroom and vision may be restricted.

Controls
No synchromesh on 3rd and 4th gears. Steering is heavy with all-terrain tyres (power steering kits can be fitted). Brake and clutch pedals require firm pressure.

A front-mounted spare wheel will impair vision for shorter drivers. Also, not good for fuel economy.

Will it fit the garage?
Maximum dimensions are:

Model	Length	Width	Height (hood up)*
80in	11ft (3.35m)	5ft 1in (1.55m)	6ft 2in (1.88m)
86in	11ft 9in (3.58m)	5ft 1in (1.55m)	6ft 4in (1.93m)
88in	11ft 11in (3.63m)	5ft 4in (1.63m)	6ft 6in (1.98m)
107in	14ft 6in (4.42m)	5ft 3in (1.60m)	7ft (2.13m)
109in	14ft 7in (4.44m)	5ft 3in (1.60m)	7ft (2.13m)

*fixed roof models are slightly lower than hooded versions

Interior space
Windscreens fold flat onto the bonnet. Seatbelts, if absent, can be fitted, though may not be legally required (eg UK pre-1964 vehicles). Interior surfaces are rugged and pet friendly. Seating capacities range from two to 12. Comfort is not an option on long journeys.

Usability
Outstanding off-road performance. Excellent load carrying ability. Series Is cannot keep up with modern traffic; later models struggle to.

Running costs
Thirsty vehicles. Series Is have the best fuel economy, if the engine is in

The spare wheel takes up significant space if mounted inside the vehicle.

good condition and well tuned. Cheaper insurance is available from agents having specialist 4x4 sections. All standard models covered in this guide are exempt from road tax in the UK.

Parts availability
Parts are often available in countries whose police or army use Series Land Rovers. USA and Australasia have suppliers. Several UK companies with websites ship parts worldwide (see Chapter 16).

Plus points
Very DIY friendly, with a variety of maintenance/repair/restoration manuals available. Relatively easily converted to alternative fuels.

Minus points
Front leaf springs mean a large turning circle, particularly for long-wheelbase models. Realistic top speeds are 55mph (88km/h) and 45mph (72km/h) for petrol- and diesel-engined vehicles respectively.

2 Cost considerations
– affordable, or a money pit?

Mechanical parts

Series	I	II/IIA
Brake shoes (x4)	x18	x18
Clutch plate	x27	x27
Dumb iron, front	x60	x25
Dynamo	x44	x44
Exhaust silencer	x36	x20
Flywheel	x120	x85
Fuel tank	x285	x80
Gasket set, engine	x65	x15
Gear selector forks	x13	x13
Head gasket set	x38	x9
Hub bearing	x10	x10
Master cylinder kit	x24	x5
Outrigger, front	x40	x18
Propshafts SWB	x50	x50
Rear crossmember	x165	x63
Shock absorber	x10	x10
Starter motor brushes	x4	x4
Timing chain	x5	x5
Trackrod	x43	x14
Trackrod end	x8	x8
Water pump	x50	x13
Wheel bearing, rear	x33	x7
Wiper blade	x10	x10
Wiper motor recon	x145	x145

Body parts

Series	I	II/IIA
Bulkhead	x895	x910
Door hinge	x9	x9
Front wing panel	x39	x34
Hood, full	x250	x230
Hood stick set	x290	x290
Lid for seatbox	x40	x10
Seatbelts, pair	x88	x88
Seat set, front	x238	x165
Wing outer	x182	x90

(Prices exclude taxes)

The 8-stud housing water pump is rare now, but can be repaired with a standard kit.

Some silencers are becoming hard to find, like this bracketed version for the Series IIA 109in Station Wagon.

A total of five different chassis lengths, four petrol engines, and two diesel engines are found across the Series I, II and IIA model range. Some parts for the 1.6-litre and the 2.6-litre petrol engines are extremely hard to find, and others are expensive. It is important to check the cost and availability of parts required to repair a known problem before buying the vehicle, particularly a Series I. If model authenticity is not an issue, then repair costs can sometimes be reduced by substituting parts from later models; even from Series III Land Rovers.

Models up to early Series IIAs have 9in clutch plates. Subsequently, 9.5in was used, and clutches became self-adjusting for wear.

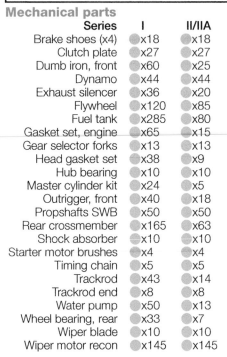

A well maintained Series I doing what it does best. It will get you where you want to go. (Courtesy Roberto Hirth)

With a large roof rack and a tow hitch fitted, you could even move house.

The Land Rover was conceived as an all-purpose vehicle with DIY potential, and this forms part of its appeal. Only its predecessor, the Jeep, is also referred to commonly by its manufacturer's name, rather than simply 'that 4x4.' You will be buying into a legend.

The youngest Series Land Rovers covered by this buyer's guide are at least four decades old. Your driving style needs to take a corresponding step backwards in time. The 1.6-litre engine will struggle to keep up with modern traffic and slows rapidly on hills. Say goodbye to concepts like acceleration, tight cornering, soft suspension, last minute braking, good fuel economy, and parallel parking. The 107in and 109in models have very wide turning circles that may affect your ability to park the vehicle exactly where you wish to. The 6-cylinder engine, if in good condition, is the only original option that allows you to reach 70mph (110km/h). Be prepared to accept a more time-dilated mode of travel, with its accent upon the journey as much as the destination.

If fuel consumption is a major concern then the diesel engine options are best, though a sound insulation kit may be advisable to facilitate conversation on long hauls. The 2-litre diesel engine is particularly under-powered; you really need to test drive it for suitability, but not many of these engines have survived. Alternatively, the relative liveliness of the petrol engines can become more economical with the fitting of an overdrive.

Volume-wise, the vehicles are spacious, though life is cramped for passengers in a 12-seater Station Wagon. It's quite amazing what can pass through the rear door of a Series Land Rover; typically 42in (1.07m) by 34in (0.86m). Towing ability is excellent, albeit on the slow side, but steep inclines will not halt you.

Not everyone wishes to leave the road behind and head overland, but if you do, it's worth bearing in mind that these vehicles were actually designed for farmer's fields. The short-wheelbase models are the preferred base vehicle for off-road competitive events, which stands testimony to their inherent ability in this regard. Their potential for performance modification is also excellent. Each country has its own policy regarding the use of un-surfaced roads, and whilst a Series Land Rover will almost always get through, you should consider the legality of doing so. The UK is gradually restricting access to vehicles on 'green lanes' and so 'pay and play' sites are becoming popular.

If you are one of the increasing number of owners who wish to retain vehicle authenticity, then modifications may be considered off-limits. In such circumstances, you may find that living with a Series IIA is less demanding on the pocket than other, earlier models. The later the year, the more change you get back when purchasing parts that are more readily available.

If, like myself, creature comforts are welcomed, then life with a Series Land Rover becomes more flexible. You can, for example, opt for a seating upgrade, fit a disc-braking kit, to make braking less of an effort, or modify the vehicle to suit your own particular needs. Some owners have even found ways to fit radios, and can actually hear the music with suitable sound insulation fitted.

For cold climates, the standard heater in all models serves for the front seat passenger to warm their hands on, and little else. If you are blessed with a tropical climate then the near vertical windscreen and vehicle sides keep the interior cooler than in many other 4x4 vehicles. The natural flow of air through the gaps in the door and floor seals is then not really a concern.

If you are mechanically minded, and can assemble flat-pack furniture without having bits left over, then you've already served a basic mechanical apprenticeship. Armed with one of the excellent workshop manuals available, you should be able to service and maintain your own vehicle. You will require a minimum of specialist tools and equipment. Many owners get great pleasure and satisfaction from maintaining and/or modifying their vehicle. There is much additional assistance available from Land Rover clubs, online websites and forums (see Chapter 17). Unlike ordinary cars, you should be able to crawl unaided under all parts of the vehicle quite easily – at least before lunch. If you do take the DIY path then it's important to realize that most of your classic vehicle's original parts are well en-route to causing you trouble. Regular inspections will pick up those hardening rubber hoses, loose joints, and leaking seals, etc. Genuine replacement parts will enable you to reach your destination, but there are many poor quality cheap alternatives that will bring your journey to a standstill. Be warned.

It is quite common for a Series I to have been assembled from different vehicles.

This is as close to original Series I design use as it gets.

Series II and IIAs have more power, better brakes, and improved interior fittings.

Campervan conversions are popular. This is a 1971 Series IIA Carawagon with roof erected, fully equipped for overland travel.

4 Relative values
– which model for you?

There is more detail on values in Chapter 12, but this chapter expresses, in percentages, the relative value of the individual models.

Series I 80in   1948-1951 1595cc petrol engine **100%**
Series I 80in   1952-1954 1997cc petrol engine **90%**
Series I 86in   1954-1956 1997cc petrol engine **85%**

Series I 107in 1954-1958 1997cc petrol engine **60%**

Series I 88in 1956-1958
1997cc petrol engine **80%**
2052cc diesel engine **75%**

Series I 109in 1956-1958 1997cc petrol engine **65%**

Series II 88in 1958-1961
2286cc petrol engine **35%**
2052cc diesel engine **35%**

Series II 109in 1958-1961 2286cc petrol engine **20%**

Series IIA 88in 1961-1971
2286cc petrol engine **30%**
2286cc diesel engine **25%**

Series IIA 109in 1961-1971
2286cc petrol engine **20%**
2625cc petrol engine (from 1967) **15%**
2286cc diesel engine **20%**

Fully restored 1948 Series I with left-hand drive. (Courtesy Roberto Hirth)

Series IIA 109in '1 ton' 1968-1971 2625cc petrol engine **20%**

Furthermore –
A well restored Series I, displaying its original factory specifications, could be a prize-winning entry in show competitions, and could command the same price as a new small family car.

It is quite common to find that an alternative engine has been fitted, in order to increase

1957 Series I 88in soft top.

A rare 1957 Series I 109in.

power and/or fuel economy. Similarly, other modifications could have been carried out, such as an LPG conversion, alloy wheels, non-standard seats or chequer-plate body panels. These modifications all detract from original specification and often lower the maximum re-sale value of a restored vehicle.

Some countries, including the UK, allow only limited modifications to vehicles before they become subject to re-appraisal for road tax purposes. A vehicle with unapproved modifications may not be worth much unless approval is granted. So check on the legal status of any modifications.

Interchangeability of parts between models means that part of the body may not be correct for the chassis number. Hybrid models are common, especially amongst vehicles that have been modified for off-road use, and their value often reflects their non-pedigree status.

1958 Series II 88in hardtop.

1968 Series IIA 88in Station Wagon.

1961 Series IIA 109in with Dormobile roof.

www.velocebooks.com / www.veloce.co.uk
Details of all current books • New book news • Special offers

5 Before you view
– be well informed

To avoid a wasted journey, and the disappointment of finding that the vehicle doesn't match your expectations, it will help if you're very clear about what questions you want to ask before you pick up the phone. Some of these points might appear basic, but when you're excited about the prospect of buying your dream classic, it's amazing how some of the most obvious things slip the mind ... Also check the current values of the model you are interested in in Land Rover magazines, which give price guides and classified ads.

Where is the car?
Is it going to be worth travelling to the next county/state, or even across a border? A locally advertised machine, although it may not sound very interesting, can add to your knowledge for very little effort, so make a visit – it might even be in better condition than expected.

Dealer or private sale?
Establish early on if the vehicle is being sold by its owner or by a trader. A private owner should have all the history, so don't be afraid to ask detailed questions. A dealer may have more limited knowledge of the vehicle's history, but should have some documentation. A dealer may offer a warranty/guarantee (ask for a printed copy), and finance.

Cost of collection and delivery?
A dealer may well be used to quoting for delivery by vehicle transporter. A private owner may agree to meet you halfway, but only agree to this after you have seen the vehicle at the vendor's address to validate the documents. Conversely, you could meet halfway and agree the sale, but insist on meeting at the vendor's address for the handover.

View – when and where?
It is always preferable to view at the vendor's home or business premises. In the case of a private sale, the vehicle's documentation should tally with the vendor's name and address. Arrange to view only in daylight, and avoid a wet day – most vehicles look better in poor light or when wet.

Reason for sale?
Do make it one of the first questions. Why is the vehicle being sold and how long has it been with the current owner? How many previous owners?

Left-hand drive to right-hand drive and special conversions
If a steering conversion has been done it can only reduce the value and it may well be that other aspects of the vehicle still reflect the specification for a foreign market. If a bodywork or LPG conversion has been carried out, was it done professionally?

Condition?
Ask for an honest appraisal of the vehicle's condition. Ask specifically about some of the check items described in Chapter 7.

All original specification?
An original equipment vehicle is invariably of higher value than a customised version

Matching data/legal ownership
Do VIN/chassis, engine numbers and licence plate match the official registration document? Is the owner's name and address recorded in the official registration documents?

For those countries that require an annual test of roadworthiness, does the vehicle have a document showing it complies (an MOT certificate in the UK, which can be verified on 0845 600 5977)?

If a smog/emissions certificate is mandatory, does the vehicle have one?

If required, does the vehicle carry a current road fund license/license plate tag?

Does the vendor own the vehicle outright? Money might be owed to a finance company or bank: the vehicle could even be stolen. Several organisations will suppl the data on ownership, based on the vehicle's licence plate number, for a fee. Such companies can often also tell you whether the vehicle has been 'written-off' by an insurance company. In the UK these organisations can supply vehicle data:

HPI – 0113 222 2010 – www.hpicheck.com

AA – 0800 056 8040 – www.theaa.com

RAC – 0330 159 0364 – www.rac.co.uk

Other countries will have similar organisations.

Unleaded fuel
If required, has the vehicle been modified to run on unleaded fuel?

Insurance
Check with your existing insurer before setting out – your current policy might not cover you if you do buy the vehicle and decide to drive it home.

How you can pay
A cheque/check will take several days to clear and the seller may prefer to sell to a cash buyer. However, a banker's draft (a cheque issued by a bank) is as good as cash, but safer, so contact your own bank and become familiar with the formalities that are necessary to obtain one.

Buying at auction?
If the intention is to buy at auction, see Chapter 10 for further advice.

Professional vehicle check (mechanical examination)
There are often marque/model specialists who will undertake professional examination of a vehicle on your behalf. Owners' clubs will be able to put you in touch with such specialists.

Other organisations that will carry out a general professional check in the UK are:

AA – 0800 085 3007 (motoring organisation with vehicle inspectors)

ABS – 0800 358 5855 (specialist vehicle inspection company)

RAC – 0870 533 3660 (motoring organisation with vehicle inspectors)

Other countries will have similar organisations.

6 Inspection equipment
– these items will really help

This book
Reading glasses (if you need them for close work)
Magnet (not powerful, a fridge magnet is ideal)
Torch
Probe (a small screwdriver works very well)
Overalls
Mirror on a stick
Digital camera
A friend, preferably a knowledgeable enthusiast

Before you rush out of the door, gather together a few items that will help as you work your way around the vehicle. This book is designed to be your guide at every step, so take it along and use the check boxes to help you assess each area of the vehicle you're interested in. Don't be afraid to let the seller see you using it.

Take your reading glasses if you need them to read documents and make close up inspections.

A magnet will help you check if the steel parts of the vehicle are full of filler. Use the magnet to sample door pillar and bulkhead areas, but be careful not to damage the paintwork. If the body panels have been repaired with filler, a magnet will not identify it because they are made from aluminium alloy. A torch with fresh batteries will be useful for peering into the wheelarches and under the vehicle.

A small screwdriver can be used – with care – as a probe, particularly on the chassis. With this you should be able to check an area of severe corrosion, but be careful – if it's really bad, the screwdriver might go right through the metal!

Be prepared to get dirty. Take along a pair of overalls, if you have them. Fixing a mirror at an angle on the end of a stick may seem odd, but you'll probably need it to help you to peer into some of the important crevices.

If you have the use of a digital camera, take it along so that you can study some areas of the vehicle more closely later. Take a picture of any part of the vehicle that causes you concern, and seek a friend's opinion. Setting the camera to high resolution, and subsequently transferring the image to a computer, will enable you to view areas in great detail.

Ideally, have a friend or knowledgeable enthusiast accompany you – a second opinion is always valuable.

7 Fifteen minute evaluation
– walk away or stay?

How does it go/sound/feel?

Concentrate on checking for the problems that would trouble your wallet/purse the most. Find out from the seller what the vehicle has been used for previously. There are advantages to poking your head into the engine bay, both before and after the test drive. When the engine is running, but still relatively cold, look for signs of a leaking water hose or a weeping radiator core. Before the engine fully warms up is also the best time to check for a smokey exhaust and miscellaneous rattles. Check if there is an oil film visible in the radiator coolant; suggesting a damaged and leaking cylinder head gasket (do not remove the radiator cap when the engine is hot). After the test drive you will have a better idea of where the almost inevitable oil leaks are;

Interiors are basic for all models It's usual to fit additional instruments.

decide for yourself whether they are significant and require urgent attention. The engine should idle smoothly without slow, heavy knocking sounds from the bottom or rapid, light chattering sounds from the top. The former would suggest worn engine bearings (bottom end) and the latter some rocker shaft component wear.

Bottom end problems are best heard when the engine is rotating quite slowly: So, with handbrake on and the engine at a fast tickover, slowly engage the clutch and listen carefully until the engine almost stalls.

Chattering sounds can be best located by using a wooden dowel or a stick as a stethoscope. If the stick leads you towards the front cover (beware of the fan blades), worn timing chain rattle could be a problem.

There shouldn't be any grey-blue or black smoke from the exhaust when the engine is revved: the former indicates combustion chamber wear, unless it occurs on start-up and when accelerating after over-run, in which case, it could be just valve stem oil seals leaking on a petrol engine. Black smoke from diesels probably means the fuel-injection needs to be tuned or replaced; whilst from petrol engines it will be a carburettor adjustment or wear problem. Acrid white smoke from a diesel engine indicates a combustion fault.

If you are insured to drive the vehicle, take it for a short road test. When starting off, listen for any initial 'clunk' sound, indicating serious wear somewhere along the transmission line.

The vehicle should drive straight 'hands-off' the steering wheel, and brake in a straight line. A small amount of steering correction to maintain a straight line is common, but you should not need to correct the steering wheel by more than the distance across the fingers of one hand. There are six steering ball joints, and wear in any one of them will affect the steering.

Try each gear for ease of use and its ability to stay selected on overrun. If 2nd or 3rd gear jumps out on over-run, the selectors may be worn.

Listen for gear chattering on over-run, indicating general wear in the gearbox.

Engaging the freewheel hubs, if they are fitted, will enable the four-wheel drive to be tested, and is also a check for front axle problems.

Don't expect a silent gearbox, though, for this age of vehicle, but gear changes should be smooth. Lack of sufficient oil can make the gearbox noisy. It's common for oil to pass through a worn seal between the main gearbox and the transfer box, resulting in the latter being overfull.

Decide whether or not any difficulty in changing down into first or second gear is due to your lack of experience in double de-clutching, as there is no synchromesh on 1st and 2nd.

Check reverse gear – you'll need to give the gear lever a firm nudge to select it.

If an overdrive has been fitted, try it out in at least 3rd gear, if road conditions permit.

Find some soft ground, preferably with a loose or gravel surface, to try the four-wheel drive and verify that it works. You won't know for sure whether the front wheels are driving unless they slip on the surface (flying gravel breaks windows!).

By checking the four-wheel drive you will also discover if the rear differential has been swapped for a more motorway-friendly version – the vehicle will handle like a wild stallion if it has, and may break a halfshaft if not released from four-wheel drive as soon as the problem is noticed. Note that, in post 1950 models covered in this guide, engaging four-wheel drive on a tarred or concrete surface, where no wheel slip is possible, can cause an axle halfshaft to break.

Be aware that the speedometer may not be the original, and that off-road mileage is much more wearing on the mechanicals than shopping trips around town – so check its history of use as far as is possible.

The cleaner the engine bay, the easier it will be to spot leaks after a test drive.

Many of these 1.6-litre engines have been replaced by larger, more powerful versions.

Exterior

A slight tilt on the vehicle to the driver's side is quite common, especially in the short-wheelbase models. This is due to the fuel tank and driver being on the same side, adding more stress to those particular springs, and so weakening them eventually.

Decide if you wish to keep the record of past off-road skirmishes. Rock sliders would have prevented this particular dimple.

The aluminium body panels do not corrode, *except* where they are joined to the chassis or other steel supports. Check the two body-mounting points on the rear crossmember for an insight into the extent of this 'electrolytic corrosion' on the vehicle.

The nature and typical lifestyle of a Series Land Rover dictates that there are likely to be some scratches and dents to the bodywork. Many enthusiasts see these as simply recording previous skirmishes off-road. You need to decide upon your own level of acceptable previous adventure souvenirs.

Under-bonnet/hood

Is it the original engine? The 2286cc petrol engine prior to 1961 had some internal weaknesses. The equivalent diesel engine with the 3-bearing crankshaft also has problems at high revs, where the crankshaft can flex and break. Can you see the engine number on the engine block? Does it agree with the one quoted in the registration document? Has off-road activity splashed battery acid around and caused serious corrosion to the battery and air filter supports or to the nearby chassis?

Underneath

All you need is a thin covering to spread on the ground to protect clothing and you can look underneath because ground clearance is at least 8in (20cm), and significantly more than this in most areas.

Examine the chassis next to and to the rear of each wheel; these parts get the water, mud and stones thrown at them. A torch may be useful here, and don't forget to feel on top of the box chassis sections. Tapping the chassis firmly with a coin should give a clear metallic ringing sound on good metal, a dull thud indicates a corroded, sound-absorbing surface. Importantly, the chassis

This stain was caused by oil from a leaking axle seal. Fluid from a leaking brake cylinder would have a similar effect.

tends to rust from the inside, where the damage cannot be seen. Outriggers and the rear chassis crossmember are usually first to require repairing, so look for signs of welding there. Any welding should appear neat and well carried out. Be wary of a chassis coated with thick underseal; these areas are best tested by gentle prodding with a screwdriver. Overlaid welded patches often conceal chassis rot and are not looked upon favourably by roadworthiness inspectors.

Look for stains on the brake backplates, which could be due to either leaking brake fluid from a brake cylinder or oil from the axle hub seal. Also look for oil leaking from the front swivel hubs. The presence of oil on the transmission brake backplate indicates that the oil seal there is damaged and will compromise the effectiveness of the brake. Oil leaks from the front of the engine and the flywheel housing are time-consuming to repair, involving higher labour charges. Expect to see some oil on the bottom of the gearbox and on the engine sump.

Suspension parts are hard to find for pre-1951 Series I models.

Interior
Lift the corners of the floor covering in the driver and passenger footwells and check for corrosion along the floor seams and the bottoms of the door pillars.

If the general condition of the seating is not to your satisfaction, it should not be a critical factor in deciding whether or not to buy, as it is replaceable.

Replacement authentic-looking seats, along with other interior fittings, are available for even the earliest Series I models.

Electrics
Has the vehicle been re-wired with a new loom? Consider it a bonus if it has; they are available for all models. The original bullet connectors tarnish and corrode, and usually work loose on cold, dark nights when it's raining! You don't have time to test the whole system, but looking at the wiring in the engine bay should give an immediate impression of how much attention the present owner has given to this important area. If the wiring is original, you could need to replace it quite soon.

Try the wiper motors to see if they are too sluggish to be effective, but do it with the engine running as voltage drops affect their performance. Wet the screen with the screen washers to view the effectiveness of the sweep. New wiper motors are expensive. If the vehicle has a dynamo rather than an alternator fitted, don't expect the heater, wipers and headlamps to all work properly at the same time – you have to choose the two you most prefer to use at any one time. Consequently, you may learn to avoid driving on cold, dark, wet nights ...

A bonus for those not craving true marque authenticity, would be if the points system in

Dynamo. An alternator supplies much more current. The conversion from dynamo to alternator is not difficult to carry out.

the distributor has been replaced by an electronic ignition system; several options are available. I remember a fellow enthusiast shaking his head in disbelief after my Series IIA started first time after three days stood idle on a wet campsite. I keep a set of old contact points for remembrance of such difficult starting problems.

Paperwork

Be aware that problem vehicles are often passed on quickly. What is the reason for sale?

If, on inspection, the vehicle still interests you, then you need to check the vehicle registration certificate; the V5C in the UK. The document details should match the vehicle you are inspecting, including engine number and chassis number. Check Chapter 17, regarding the 2286cc engines, for details on various issues related to the interchangeability of engine blocks and cylinder heads. If you are examining the vehicle at a location that is not the registered address, you should be satisfied as to why that is the case. In the United Kingdom, the person named on the V5C is the registered keeper, and is not legally required to be the actual owner.

Chassis numbers are mostly located on the right-hand front spring hanger (otherwise known as the dumb iron). For 80in models, the chassis number should be on the left-side engine mounting, but even if the original mounting is still present, it's probably unreadable by now. A replacement galvanized chassis will not have a number, and neither will a replacement dumb iron, unless it has been re-stamped by the owner. An original chassis number plate should be present on either the inner or outer bulkhead.

If the vehicle has been modified significantly, check that these modifications are approved by the DVLA (for UK residents) so as to retain age-related road tax exemption.

Is it worth staying longer?

• Is the colour what you expected?
• Is the condition of the paintwork acceptable to you?
• Are you confident you can identify and repair any faults you have found, or do you need a second opinion?
• Are the main mechanical components in reasonable working order?
• Are any problems you have discovered reflected in the sale price?
• Is your heart ruling your head?
• Maybe you need to refer to a marque specialist, rather than act in haste and repent at leisure.

Fully restored early Series I vehicles are much sought-after and admired. Don't expect to recover your restoration costs, though, if you sell.

8 Key points
– where to look for problems

Key points are focussed around the problems that would cost the most to rectify. For all Series I, II and IIA models, this involves thoroughly checking the chassis, bulkhead, engine, and gearbox. Getting these items repaired professionally may require budgeting for more than the initial cost of the vehicle itself. If you are carrying out all the work yourself, it will be time-consuming and you may need to budget for specialist tools and lifting gear. In some locations it may be possible to hire the necessary equipment. Some countries have low labour charges, but these can be offset by the cost of having bulky items shipped out to you from the UK or elsewhere.

This galvanized chassis is already over two decades old, but shows no sign of corrosion of the vulnerable outriggers.

Water thrown into the chassis dumb irons rots them from inside. Stress from the leaf spring accelerates the corrosion.

The rear chassis crossmember corrodes under the mud that often accumulates here. Keep this area clean.

The corner bulkhead is very prone to corrosion. Note the signs of a possibly weak repair here. Replacement inserts are available for welding in. Use a magnet in this area.

This inside corner bulkhead is corroded through. Check this area carefully; it supports the upper door hinge.

The footwells and front door pillars form part of the bulkhead. They rot at their lowest points. Remove floor covering to inspect.

Door pillars rot from the inside. This one has been amateur welded, and body filler used to level the surface. Be wary. A replacement lower door pillar section can be welded in – not a major job.

Oil spraying from the crankcase breather indicates worn valve guides/cylinder bores and/or piston rings It occurs mainly at high engine revs.

9 Serious evaluation
– 60 minutes for years of enjoyment

Score each section as follows: 4 = excellent; 3 = good; 2 = average; 1 = poor
The totting up procedure is detailed at the end of the chapter. Be realistic in your
marking!

It's hard to remember all
the details of a vehicle
you inspect, even an hour
or two later, so circle the
Excellent, Good, Average
or Poor box of each
section as you go along.
The vehicle evaluation
procedure has been
planned with the efficient
use of your time in mind.
The intended order is;
external inspection,
underneath examination

If professional re-painting is
required, having the bodywork
stripped down and surfaces
repaired will be costly.

Check alignment along
the line of body panel
cappings. Problems
may be from poor
assembly or a wrongly
welded outrigger.

from front to rear, under bonnet/hood inspection,
internal assessment, test drive and, finally, a follow-up
assessment.

Paintwork

☐4 ☐3 ☐2 ☐1

If you wish to display the vehicle at shows you may
prefer a professionally done authentic-to-the-year paint
job. Or, working in a remote jungle area, brush-painted
Hammerite may be sufficient. Your requirements probably
fall somewhere between these extremes. Decide upon
what quality of paintwork is appropriate to you and score
the vehicle accordingly. A professional paint job will last a
long time and could prove a good investment. If, however,
you prefer to go down the DIY route, then year- and

Body filler may have
been used to cover
up dents, but off-road
activity stresses it.

model-specific paint is available
to either spray, brush on or
apply with a roller. You need a
larger-than-average garage if you plan to do the painting
yourself indoors.
• Assess the condition of paintwork

Body panels

☐4 ☐3 ☐2 ☐1

On Land Rovers of this age group, you are more likely to
find dents than corrosion; the body panels are aluminium

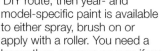

The body panels are all made from an aluminium alloy
called 'Birmabright.'

and the alloy is weaker than steel. Body panels are secured to a steel frame, and yes, this frame does rust. Some panels are becoming hard to find, especially for the 107in.

Some alloy panels are fixed together with steel bolts; these two dissimilar metals interact, so that the alloy around the fixing point corrodes. This is often the reason why a wing panel, for example, may appear a little loose, resulting in it rattling on rough ground.

Wings without headlamp inserts are becoming scarce.

As mentioned, the traditional method of using a weak magnet to detect the presence of body filler, will not work on the alloy panels. However, it's comforting to know that a panel will not have been body-filled because of corrosion problems, but probably simply to have saved the trouble of panel beating the metal back into shape – not easily achieved with 'Birmabright' alloy.

• Check the general condition of all panels

Front wings/fenders   4️⃣ 3️⃣ 2️⃣ 1️⃣

Not usually a problem area. In post 1968/69 Series IIAs, check for corrosion of the headlamp bowls fitted into the wings, as they are more prone to road spray in this location. Also check:
• The mudshield at the rear of the wing
• The mounting of the wing panels to the bulkhead pillars
• Radiator support frame

The radiator support frame is prone to rust, especially along the bottom edge where it supports the bonnet and wings

Wheels   4️⃣ 3️⃣ 2️⃣ 1️⃣

• Gripping a wheel at both sides and rocking it firmly, whilst the axle is supported safely on a stand, will identify any play due to worn wheel bearings. If grasped at the top and bottom, any play will either confirm worn wheel bearings or, on front wheels, indicate worn swivel pins. Early Series I rear wheel bearings are expensive and somewhat troublesome to replace
• If original wheels are fitted, check for corrosion along the central grooved depression
• Check the wheel nut mounting flanges on the spare wheel for severe corrosion. You'll have to assume the other four wheels are in a similar condition

Dangerously corroded wheel securing flanges are often ignored.

Tyres   4️⃣ 3️⃣ 2️⃣ 1️⃣

235/70/R16 and 235/85/R16 are large enough and relatively fuel economical for short-wheelbase and long-wheelbase vehicles, respectively. Aggressive tread gives good off-road performance, but lowers fuel economy on the road and makes the steering heavy.

- Assess the tyres relative to your intended use
- Are tyre treads legal and the walls without cracks?

Do the tyres suit your requirements for road, off-road, or all-terrain?

Windscreen

Its ability to fold flat provides a useful facility on all models in tropical climates. Usually, however, the hinges have long ago seized solid.
- Does the windscreen fold flat against the bonnet/hood?
- Check for any glass damage in the driver's field of vsion (can be a roadworthiness certificate failure)

Owners of soft top models are most likely to fold the windscreen flat.

Door shut lines

Stand at the rear of a closed door and look along the vertical door line:
- Is there a uniform space down the full height of the door?
- Does a glazed door bend out a little at the top? This would indicate corrosion at the joint between the upper and lower sections of the door, where they are bolted together. Rear passenger doors on long-wheelbase models are especially susceptible to this fault. Mounting the spare wheel on the rear door of a Station Wagon can distort the door frame over time

If the door bends outward at the bottom, the internal steel support frame is likely to be corroded.

Doors

The door skins are Birmabright alloy and will not show corrosion, but the internal frames and door pillars are steel. If no trim is present, you can inspect the steel door frames. Series I doors are prone to cracking.

Water sits in the steel window channels, encourages mould, and rots them. The rot then progresses down the steel door frame. Replacement channel and complete door tops are available. Keeping drain holes clear under the windows is important. Series I doors often fit badly, but new hinges are available.

Water usually rots out the lower door frames.

• Inspect the surface of closing edges, especially where the lower and upper door sections join on Series II and IIAs.
• With each door half open, lift it up, feeling for wear in the hinges
• Carefully feel along the bottom edges of the doors for corrosion

Door trim   4️⃣ 3️⃣ 2️⃣ 1️⃣

If there is door trim (most Series Is never had it; in which case, assess the visible door frame).
• Assess the trim's condition, especially near the bottom where water will have leaked inside the door. Replacements are available, even in authentic-looking 'elephant hide' vinyl

Sill channels/rockers   4️⃣ 3️⃣ 2️⃣ 1️⃣

These are hidden from view on Series II and IIA models by the sill panels, and are subject to rotting, especially at the ends. In four-door

Replacement steel door frame sections are available. Cut to length and weld into place as needed.

models, check under the middle door pillar. Replacements are available but time-consuming to weld-in.
• Check general condition

Series Is don't have cosmetic sill panels.

Body attachment points   4️⃣ 3️⃣ 2️⃣ 1️⃣

These can be seen without getting underneath the vehicle. You will probably find some corrosion here, but it should only be minor and around the points where the aluminium body is joined to the chassis. Measures were taken at the design stage to minimise this 'electrolytic corrosion' by using various materials to separate the two interacting metals.

Check in particular:
• Where the rear body is bolted to the rear chassis crossmember
• Where the centre body is bolted to the chassis outriggers

A sill channel has been fabricated from heavy-duty shelving supports.

Aluminium angle has been used here to repair a corroded aluminium floor section.

If the body panel is stressed, corrosion can spread away from the attachment point and along the line of stress.

Door pillars

Water rots them from inside the channel sections, especially the bottom ends – see the photo in Chapter 8. Replacement pillar sections are available to be welded-in. Check:
• The regions above and below where the hinges are attached on all side doors
• The sloping part of the pillar on rear side passenger doors for the 107in and 109in models

Flooring

For any flooring that is thick aluminium alloy and screwed down, check:
• The areas around the floorpanel fixing screws for corrosion of the panels or of their steel mating surfaces
• The horizontal alloy flanges on the seat base for corrosion – caused by a combination of stress and the steel fixing screws
• The driver and passenger side footwells for corrosion, especially along seams and where bolted to floorpanels
• The footwell around where the headlamp dipswitch is mounted
• The lower edges of the steel gearbox diaphragm cover

Rear sloping door pillars rot. This one has been poorly repaired by riveting.

Remove all this floor covering to inspect the floorpanels.

Bulkhead/dash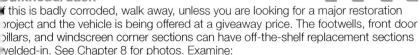

If this is badly corroded, walk away, unless you are looking for a major restoration project and the vehicle is being offered at a giveaway price. The footwells, front door pillars, and windscreen corner sections can have off-the-shelf replacement sections welded-in. See Chapter 8 for photos. Examine:
• The upper footwell area, not checked earlier
• From inside the vehicle, the area between the parcel shelf and the door pillar on the driver and passenger sides
• The area just below the windscreen (difficult to repair)
• From outside the vehicle, the corners just below the windscreen on each side of the vehicle

Checking under the vehicle

Normally, to check under a car, it's recommended to either pre-book time on a

A 3ft (1m) wide roll of old carpet, or similar, helps to keep clothes clean – though overalls are advisable.

garage lift, if available locally, or to get out the jack and axle stands. However, if you are able to 'tread lightly' on your bathroom scales, all Series I, II and IIA models can be inspected from underneath, without lifting gear, due to their large ground clearance. I find I leave less of my DNA on the chassis, etc, if I wear some form of simple headgear!

Chassis
4 3 2 1

If the original chassis is still fitted, try to find and read the chassis number: on Series Is it should be present on the left-hand side engine mounting or left-hand rear spring hanger; on Series II and IIAs, look on the outer edge of the right-hand side front dumb iron. Corrosion and paint may have rendered the number unreadable. Try to read as many consecutive digits as possible and note them down.

Tapping the chassis with a small screwdriver and listening for a metallic ring or dead thud reveals the state of the chassis, as much internally as externally. Corrosion tends to occur from the inside since moisture stays there longer.

Be aware, whilst checking under the vehicle, that loose and hanging brake pipes which can vibrate, can lead to stress fractures – so look out for any.

Check the following on each side of the vehicle (see Chapter 8 for photos):
• Front dumb iron
• Integrity of any visible repairs, such as welded patches
• Outriggers
• Lowest parts of the chassis
• Sides and top around the rear wheel area
• Rear crossmember

In the UK, a replacement chassis should be reported to the DVLA, so it can issue a new official chassis number.

Wear in springs usually begins near the shackles, where stress is greatest.

Front axle
4 3 2 1

A thin film of oil or graphite lubricant between the spring leaves helps reduce friction and corrosion and indicates a dedicated owner. Be aware that:
• Rear spring hangers should be almost vertical. The individual leaves of each spring should be parallel to each other, not splayed apart
• Any oil or brake fluid stains on the lower part of a brake backplate indicates a leaking oil seal or faulty brake cylinder
• If the chrome swivel hubs on the front axle are not hidden by leather gaiters, their

A steering damper was available as an optional extra on the Series IIA.

Leaf springs for early Series Is are narrower than for later models.

surfaces should be smooth and not pitted. There shouldn't be any oil leaking from this large seal; as evidenced by oil having reached the lower swivel arm fixing bolts. Sand and mud trapped under the swivel seal erodes the chrome surface. Leaking hubs can be concealed by using swivel hub grease in place of the recommended oil. Swivel housings are time-consuming and expensive to replace. Series II and IIA swivel housings fit Series I axles

Inspecting the floor where the vehicle is normally parked could reveal this rear differential oil leak.

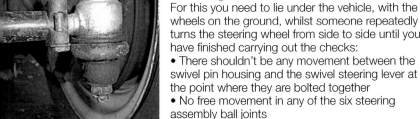

Original ball joints have nipples. They can be greased to remain serviceable for longer.

Oil leaks

It is common for the lower engine sump area to display signs of oil leaking from somewhere. It's a good idea to wipe clean the area after inspecting it, and check again after the test drive. The following sources of oil leaks are more difficult and costly to repair:
• Behind the crankshaft pulley at the front of the engine
• The rear lower surface of the cylinder head
• Where the front propshaft joins the differential housing

Steering

For this you need to lie under the vehicle, with the wheels on the ground, whilst someone repeatedly turns the steering wheel from side to side until you have finished carrying out the checks:
• There shouldn't be any movement between the swivel pin housing and the swivel steering lever at the point where they are bolted together
• No free movement in any of the six steering assembly ball joints
• No oil leaking out of the bottom of the steering relay
• If a steering damper has been fitted, consider it a bonus

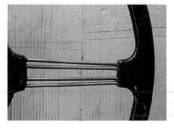

Heavy off-road use may have caused dangerous cracks near the spokes. Expensive to replace, though they can be refurbished.

Shock absorbers

④ ③ ② ①

There isn't a practical way of testing these, except that you can look for leakage of oil on their sides.

This front shock absorber has had oil from a leaking axle joint blown onto it.

Gearbox

④ ③ ② ①

Check for oil leaks in the following places:
• A slight amount of oil leaking from the drain hole in the flywheel housing is not unusual, but it means that the crankshaft rear oil seal will need attention in the future. The gearbox or engine will need to be removed in order to replace the seal
• Oil on the lower gearbox usually means the oil filler cap is leaking, as it's only held down by a spring and the cork joint washer often doesn't give a good seal
• Any oil around the junction of the front propshaft with the gearbox will be coming from the front output shaft oil seal
• Oil stains on the drum of the transmission brake means the rear output shaft oil seal is leaking, and oil could get onto the transmission brake linings

Propshafts

④ ③ ② ①

• With freewheel hubs engaged (if fitted), there should be less than a quarter-turn of free play on the front propshaft
• With the handbrake off and wheels chocked, perform the same test on the rear propshaft

Rear axle

④ ③ ② ①

It's OK if spring leaves are horizontal, but not bent downwards. A full set of radial tyres and parabolic springs improve the ride, especially on short-wheelbase models. Perform these checks for each end of the axle:
• The rear spring hanger should be at approximately 45 degrees, and the individual leaves of the spring all parallel to each other, not splayed apart

The breather valve on top of the axle should be kept clean and clear to reduce axle oil leaks caused by pressure build-up.

• Any sign of oil or brake fluid stains on the lower part of the brake backplate indicates a leaking oil seal or faulty brake cylinder

Consider a reinforced axle, like this, a bonus.

Exhaust system

Cracked exhaust manifold mounting flanges are expensive to repair and a replacement manifold is not cheap, when available.

Exhausts corrode internally at their lowest points, and externally behind wheels.

Series Is usually have exhaust heat shields fitted to protect tyres and the passenger seatbase compartment.

• Check the entire system for corrosion and for good flexible mountings. Only award an 'Excellent' rating if a stainless steel system is fitted

• Inspect the inside of the tailpipe for a powdery black deposit, indicating an over rich fuel mixture. Ideally, it should be light grey

Fuel tank(s)

Water-contaminated fuel or condensation in an empty tank can cause corrosion from the inside. Off-road driving, with perished rubber tank mountings, can stress corroded seams and cause leakage – in the case of petrol, detectable by smell rather than by sight. They are not practical to repair and rear-mounted tanks can be very expensive to replace.

• Check for leakage

Auxillary tanks may have been fitted, like this one, under the passenger seat.

This rear body support strut above the fuel tank has a large corrosion hole.

Mechanical aspects

If the spare wheel is mounted on the bonnet, check the security of the fastenings on the bonnet prop rod before poking your head inside the engine bay. If there isn't a wheel there, it only takes a few seconds to disconnect the prop rod and hold the bonnet back against the windscreen for easier inspection.

Cooling system   4 3 2 1

If there is water movement in the radiator neck on starting a cold engine, the thermostat is missing.
• Check for signs of water leaking through the vanes of the radiator and the top and bottom sealing joints
• Remove the radiator cap and look for any oil film; if present, the cylinder head gasket is probably about to fail
• Feel under the top fanbelt pulley (engine not running!) for water from a leaking water pump

A corroded and enlarged air hole in the cap allows moist air to enter and contaminate fluid.

Engine & ancillaries   4 3 2 1

If a V8 engine has been fitted, check that the brakes and suspension have been suitably upgraded to match the performance.

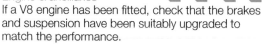

Engine mounts should not be perished or cracked.

Pre-1961 2286cc petrol engines had some internal weaknesses. Cast iron cylinder heads on diesels are prone to cracking. 7:1 and 8:1 compression ratio cylinder heads are interchangeable on the 2286cc petrol engine. The ratio is stamped on the cylinder head.
• On petrol engines, check the carburettor spindle for wear by turning it and wriggling it in all directions. If sideways movement is present, the carburettor will leak fuel and subsequently need replacing (Zenith 34ICH is prone to this fault)
• If you are aiming at an authentic restoration according to year and model, check what parts you may wish to replace, even though they may be perfectly serviceable at present (such as the air cleaner, carburettor, and dynamo)

Miscellaneous engine bay mechanicals   4 3 2 1

• Up to early Series IIA, check the condition of the combined brake and clutch fluid reservoir for corrosion

The engine number is located on this vertical rectangular surface next to the exhaust

Additional connections to the fusebox or elsewhere should have soldered spade ends, not just be crimped onto the bare wire.

- Check the steering box and relay are both securely attached to the chassis (especially Series I)
- Some vehicles will have been fitted with an oil cooler by a previous owner. Check for leaks, and be aware that this engine has probably had a hard life at some point in the past because oil coolers are not required for normal operation
- Whilst you have your head in the engine bay, make a note of the engine number; it's stamped vertically on a smooth section of the engine block near the exhaust outlet and the water pump housing

The wiring loom

Electrical problems are common on older vehicles, as the insulation becomes brittle and cracks, also the bullet and spade end connections become corroded and work loose. Amateur installations are common and should be treated with scepticism. New looms are available for all models. Distributors for early Series Is are expensive to repair, even caps for the 1.6-litre version are not cheap. Check:

The main loom and all its extensions are secured to the body, engine or chassis as appropriate, to prevent chafing
- If the loom is the original wiring – score 'Poor' for this section
- Additional wires – for added instruments or extra lighting, etc – have been fitted with secondary insulation, in a similar manner to the main loom, and are of the correct electrical load rating

Ignition timing will never be accurate if the central shaft is worn and can be moved laterally at all.

If the distributor has some type of electronic ignition fitted, consider it a bonus.

Unleaded fuel conversion

For petrol engines, ask to see written evidence that the cylinder head has had the original valve seats replaced with hardened ones. New valves should have been fitted at the same time; it's a costly conversion. Failure to convert the valve seats will shorten the life of the cylinder head. It will be several thousand miles before deterioration in engine performance becomes apparent, though.

Several companies in the UK convert Series Land Rovers to LPG for better fuel economy. DIY kits are also available.

Chassis & engine number 4 3 2 [

It's now time to enter the vehicle. You should first check the VIN plate, usually fixed to the bulkhead above the gearbox tunnel, but location does vary according to model. Does the number match the one you may have found earlier on the chassis? Does it agree with the one recorded on the vehicle registration document? Note that these VIN plates are also available as blanks so inspect the plate for age characteristics. The UK's V5C form is printed on paper with distinctive watermarks.

Internal facilities 4 3 2 1

• If it's a hooded vehicle, and the hood is available, make sure you see it fully erected
• If seatbelts are fitted (they are not a legal requirement in pre-1973 UK-registered vehicles), check the condition of them and their mountings
• Has a sound insulation kit been fitted (a bonus on diesels!)? If yes, and it has been stuck to the floor, mark down as it restricts floor inspection

Inspect hoods for tears, cracks and the integrity of the window, if one is present. Replacements are available.

Internal aesthetics 4 3 2 1

If you are purchasing for serious off-road use, don't allow a neat and tidy interior trim to eclipse the significance of any mechanical failings that you may have already spotted. On the other hand, if you are developing a liking for the vehicle but the interior or soft hood is poor, be aware that these trim items are all available, even in the original authentic style, if required.

• Is it to your liking?

Early Series Is only had internal door handles. These flaps are needed to access them from outside.

Original style side-steps like these are scarce now

Test drive
Provided you are insured and the vehicle is road legal, take it for a 30min test drive. This is the only satisfactory way to assess some important mechanical aspects of the vehicle. If you are only insured for third party claims, then you may wish to inform the seller of this fact.

Instruments/warning lights

The standard instruments are very basic and limited in scope. It's common for owners to have added oil pressure and water temperature gauges themselves.
- Check the effectiveness of all gauges fitted, and use their information to assess the engine's condition as you continue through the test drive
- The green oil warning light should illuminate with ignition on, and quickly extinguish when the engine starts
- If a heater is fitted, check if the fan operates. You could check the amount of heat produced during or after the test drive. A replacement Smiths-type round heater matrix is expensive. Early Series Is had a Clayton heater as an optional extra

Engine start
The present owner will best advise on throttle and/or choke settings according to present weather conditions.
- Does the starter gear engage fully with the flywheel? Does it sound like there is a worn starter dog, or even missing flywheel teeth?
- Does the engine start easily?

Engine core plugs can corrode from the inside and leak. Easy to renew.

Engine sounds
The 2286cc petrol engine is known to suffer from timing chain rattle. Diesel engines need about 30sec of glow plug pre-heating to start.
- The engine should idle reasonably smoothly; allowing for understandable accumulated wear in moving components. If you feel that idling is a little too erratic, check it again after the test drive. A multi-meter with tachometer capability is useful here
- If there is a metallic rattle from the top of the engine, indicating tappet problems, check again after the test drive; if still present then mark down, but this problem is not expensive or difficult to fix
- Listen for dull knocking sounds from low in the engine; if present then crankshaft bearings or even a worn crankshaft is likely
- Check the exhaust smoke when the

A 'clunk' when driving over a bump could mean a worn roadspring or chassis rubber bush. Rubber perishes more rapidly in tropical climates.

engine is revved a little from idling: if blueish, the pistons and/or rings are worn; if black, the fuel mixture is too rich for petrol, or the injection system needs an overhaul on a diesel (can be expensive)

If the engine doesn't rank highly on this section, and you found oil leaks in the earlier 'oil leaks' test, it's probably time to walk away. 2286cc engines have a longer life than the 1.6- or 2-litre versions. Some spares for the 2.6-litre are becoming hard to find.

Lights

• Switch on the headlamps and check the reading on the ammeter as you do so. Even a dynamo should be able to keep the ignition warning light off, provided no other electrical items are on at the same time
• Do all the other lights and indicators work?

Completely original lighting is potentially dangerous on busy modern roads. The bulbs at least should be upgraded.

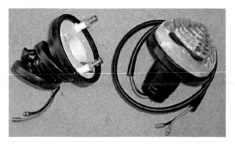

Corroded sidelight and indicator light mountings can be replaced with rubber versions.

Early Series Is had the side lights here.

Dashboard ancillary items

Before setting off on the test drive, check the operation of the windscreen wipers and screen washers. Check the sweep of the blades and the speed of the wiper motor (engine running). The wiper motor is expensive to replace or overhaul.

Screen washers of this vintage often need priming a few times before delivering the goods.

Original instrumentation is basic. Consider performance diagnostic instruments a bonus

Optional interior extra items

Possibilities include, but not for all models: heater/demister, heated windscreen, flyscreens, and radio.

• Assess whatever extras are present

Big heater, but only warm air for the passenger's benefit; a little is ducted to the windscreen for demisting.

Brake pedal operation

80in models require a novel pedal action that needs practice.

If you are not satisfied with the first two brake checks below, don't continue with a test drive. Series I brake linkage is often in poor condition, but parts are available for substitution from later models, if needed.

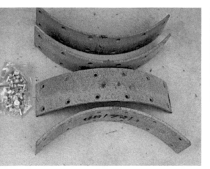

Brake lining kits are sometimes available when new brake shoes are not.

Uneven wear on brake shoes, as here, can cause the vehicle to pull to one side when braking.

• The brake pedal should be firm on initially applying pressure, and should not travel more than halfway to the floor before stopping
• Check the brake master cylinder seals by repeatedly pressing gently on the brake pedal; a good seal will allow the pedal to come to rest at the same point each time. Also apply continuous pressure on the pedal and see if the pedal gradually creeps down at all, or remains firm
• Do the brakes inspire confidence? Do they require excessive pedal pressure? Bare in mind there will probably be no servo assistance, except on later Series IIA models. Note that all models with the pendant-style brake pedal can be converted to servo assisted, if desired
• Does the vehicle stop in a straight line? If it doesn't then it could be due to a partially seized brake cylinder or fluid on the brake linings
• Any scraping sounds on braking suggest badly worn brake linings. Note that temporary brake squeal, heard on braking, is common when the brake drum edges are corroded and grit gets inside it. Brake fade can be due to glazed brake linings and polished brake drums. The glaze can be broken as a cure, instead of replacing components

Clutch assessment

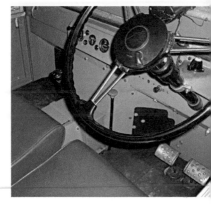

These checks are with the vehicle stationary:

• Depress the clutch pedal to the floor. There shouldn't be any squealing sounds, which would indicate a worn clutch release bearing – cheap to buy, but expensive or time-consuming to fit

• Try selecting first gear. If difficult to select, a worn clutch is possible, but it could also be worn gear selector forks

• Does the clutch engage when the pedal is about halfway up its travel arc? The clutch became self-adjusting with early Series IIAs

• Does the clutch engage smoothly, without juddering?

¾ inch (2cm) of pedal free play should be present for the early mechanical clutch mechanism.

Gearbox assessment

• Does the gearbox sound chattery on over-run in any gear?

• Does the gearbox jump out of any gear when, after accelerating, you release the accelerator suddenly?

These are indications of general gearbox wear. A replacement gearbox is usually more economical than a complete overhaul of the existing one.

Four-wheel drive

The only sure way to test this is to find a loose gravely surface, engage freewheeling hubs if fitted, and see if the front wheels spin. Check both high and low transmission gearboxes. There should be no unhealthy sounds. If four-wheel drive cannot be selected, it will probably just be a linkage problem.

Depressing the yellow knob selects 4WD. Pulling the red lever rearwards whilst stationary selects low ratio 4WD. To de-select high ratio 4WD, pull the red lever rearwards and then return it.

Steering

The Series I-style steering wheel and horn push are expensive.

• 'Clonk' sounds from near a front wheel, on turning sharp corners, could be loose U-bolts or worn suspension bushes

• Does the vehicle steer straight without the

Earlier models than this had the horn push on a bracket mounted on the steering column.

need for constant correction? Note that if crossply tyres are fitted, steering will tend to follow grooves in the road. Remember that steering needs to pass the test for a roadworthiness certificate. Series I steering boxes are expensive to replace or recondition
• Does the steering self-centre after cornering? This indicates that the swivel hubs are lubricated and adjusted correctly
   It is common for quite violent shaking to occur after hitting a pothole on models where a steering damper is not fitted. Steering damper kits are available.

Adjustment of these steering lock stops will prevent wide tyres from fouling the springs.

Transmission/parking brake

• If both a gentle slope and a steep incline are available, try the former first for

handbrake efficiency. Otherwise, with high ratio first gear selected and the handbrake on, try moving off gently. If forward movement is possible, either oil from the gearbox has contaminated the transmission brake linings or the mechanism needs adjustment
• Park on a decline, then release the transmission brake. If there is reluctance to move forwards, the transmission shoes can be binding. Check again using the footbrake and if the same occurs, the wheel brake shoes are binding. The latter is easily verified by feeling for warmth in the steel wheels after a short drive

Operation of this brake whilst the vehicle is in motion can cause transmission damage.

Overdrive (if fitted)

Series III Land Rovers (outside the scope of this guide) had the option of a factory-fitted Fairey overdrive unit. These units were also obtainable from the manufacturer, and subsequently fitted by many owners of Series I, II and IIA models. Units and parts are now re-manufactured. Secondhand original units are often seriously worn. If an overdrive is fitted and working satisfactorily, mark as 'Excellent.' Rocky Mountain make a Roverdrive overdrive to fit these models.

Performance assessment

• Did the engine rev well at the top end

A Weber conversion kit is available as an economical alternative to the Solex or Zenith carburettors, though power is reduced.

of the range, indicating a well tuned ignition system, or fade off and loose power too early?

• Given a suitable stretch of level road, it should be possible to reach 60mph with al models that are in good condition and well tuned, though a Series I would struggle to reach it, even on a 747 runway!

Seating

• On completion of the test drive, evaluate how you felt in terms of comfort, ease of operation of the controls, and all round visibility. Station Wagons are easiest to fit alternative seating. Remember that seating installation must satisfy requirements of a road safety test

Seating capability varies across the model range, from 3 to 12 people.

Engine health

Leave the engine running and check:

• The tappets are not significantly noisier than they were when idling before the test drive

• The inside of the oil vent cap from the rocker cover for a creamy deposit, indicating a head gasket problem

• Signs of oil splattering from the oil filler cap and back pressure at the rocker cover vent, indicating a worn engine (see Chapter 8 for photo)

Each vehicle you look at will have been personalised to some degree.
Is it to your taste?

External aesthetics

4 3 2 1

The vehicle may be still baring off-road driving scars. If it's a soft top model, check if the perspex windows have become brittle and cracked.

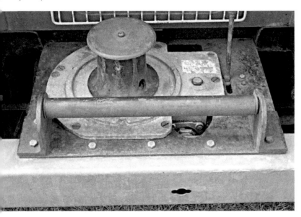

• Is the front bumper damaged?
• Are the rear corners damaged?
• Are the wheels standard and in good condition or, if alloy rims have been fitted, will these suit any off road requirements you may have?

The capstan winch is engine driven, so doesn't require a battery.

Ancillary equipment

A wide variety of off-road or utility equipment may have been fitted, such as a winch, roof-rack, tow hitch, chequer-plate body panels, underbody protection guards, additional lighting, etc.

Score the equipment present according to its particular appeal to you.

A rear power take-off is the icing on the cake for an authentic restoration project.

Roadworthy test certificate

You need to look at the most recent roadworthy test certificate and see if any recommendations for further improvement have been recorded on it. Note that the number of countries prohibiting the registration of older vehicles for use on public roads is increasing.

Evaluation procedure

Add up the total points.
Score: 204 = excellent; 153 = good; 102 = average; 51 = poor.

A vehicle scoring over 143 should be completely usable and require the minimum of repair, although continued maintenance and care will be required to keep it in condition. Vehicles scoring between 51 and 104 will require a full restoration – the cost of which will be much the same, regardless of points scored. Vehicles scoring between 105 and 142 points will require very careful assessment of the necessary repair/restoration costs in order to arrive at a realistic purchase price.

www.velocebooks.com / www.veloce.co.uk
Details of all current books • New book news • Special offers

10 Auctions
– sold! Another way to buy your dream

Auction pros & cons

Pros: Prices will usually be lower than those of dealers or private sellers, and you might grab a real bargain on the day. Auctioneers have usually established clear title with the seller. At the venue you can usually examine documentation relating to the vehicle.

Cons: You have to rely on a sketchy catalogue description of condition and history. The opportunity to inspect is limited, and you cannot drive the car. Auction cars are often a little below par and may require some work. It's easy to overbid. There will usually be a buyer's premium to pay in addition to the auction hammer price.

Which auction?

Auctions by established auctioneers are advertised in car magazines and on the auction houses' websites. A catalogue, or a simple printed list of the lots for auction, might only be available a day or two ahead, though often lots are listed and pictured on auctioneers' websites much earlier. Contact the auction company to ask if previous auction selling prices are available as this is useful information (details of past sales are often available on websites).

Catalogue, entry fee, & payment details

When you purchase the catalogue of the vehicles in the auction, it often acts as a ticket allowing two people to attend the viewing days and the auction. Catalogue details tend to be comparatively brief, but will include information such as 'one owner from new, low mileage, full service history', etc. It will also usually show a guide price to give you some idea of what to expect to pay, and will tell you what is charged as a 'Buyer's premium.' The catalogue will also contain details of acceptable forms of payment. At the fall of the hammer an immediate deposit is usually required, the balance payable within 24 hours. If you plan to pay by cash note that there may be a cash limit. Some auctions will accept payment by debit card; and sometimes credit or charge cards are acceptable, but will often incur an extra charge. A bank draft or bank transfer will have to be arranged in advance with your own bank as well as with the auction house. No vehicle will be released before all payments are cleared. If delays occur in payment transfers then storage costs can accrue.

Buyer's premium

A buyer's premium will be added to the hammer price: don't forget this in your calculations. It's not usual for there to be a further state tax or local tax on the purchase price and/or on the buyer's premium.

Viewing

In some instances it's possible to view on the day, or days, before, as well as in the hours prior to the auction. Auction officials may be willing to help out by opening engine and luggage compartments and may allow you to inspect the interior. While the officials may start the engine for you, a test drive is out of the question. Crawling under and around the vehicle as much as you want is permitted, but you can't suggest that the vehicle you are interested in be jacked up, or attempt to do the job yourself. You can also ask to see any documentation available.

Bidding

Before you take part in the auction, decide on your maximum bid – and stick to it!

It may take a while for the auctioneer to reach the lot you're interested in, so use that time to observe how other bidders behave. When it's the turn of your car, attract the auctioneer's attention and make an early bid. The auctioneer will then look to you for a reaction every time another bid is made; usually the bids will be in fixed increments until the bidding slows, whereupon smaller increments will often be accepted before the hammer falls. If you want to withdraw from the bidding, make sure the auctioneer understands your intentions – a vigorous shake of the head when he or she looks to you for the next bid should do the trick!

Assuming that you are the successful bidder, the auctioneer will note your card or paddle number, and from that moment on you will be responsible for the vehicle.

If the vehicle is unsold, either because it failed to reach the reserve or because there was little interest, it may be possible to negotiate with the owner, via the auctioneer, after the sale is over.

Successful bid

There are two more items to think about: how to get the vehicle home; and insurance. If you can't drive the car, your own or a hired trailer is one way, another is to have the vehicle shipped using the facilities of a local company. The auction house will also have details of companies specialising in the transfer of vehicles.

Insurance for immediate cover can usually be purchased on site, but it may be more cost-effective to make arrangements with your own insurance company in advance, and then call to confirm the full details.

eBay & other online auctions

eBay and other online auctions could land you a vehicle at a bargain price, though you'd be foolhardy to bid without examining the vehicle first, something most vendors encourage. A useful feature of eBay is that the geographical location of the vehicle is shown, so you can narrow your choices to those within a realistic radius of home. Be prepared to be outbid in the last few moments of the auction. Remember your bid is binding, and it will be very, very difficult to get restitution in the case of a crooked vendor fleecing you – caveat emptor!

Be aware that some cars offered for sale in online auctions are 'ghost' cars. Don part with any cash without being sure that the vehicle does actually exist and is as described (usually pre-bidding inspection is possible).

Auctioneers

Barrett-Jackson www.barrett-jackson.com
Bonhams www.bonhams.com
British Car Auctions (BCA) www.bca-europe.com or www.british-car-auctions.co.uk
Cheffins www.cheffins.co.uk
Christies www.christies.com
Coys www.coys.co.uk
Dorset Vintage and Classic Auctions www.dvca.co.uk
eBay www.ebay.com
H&H www.classic-auctions.co.uk
RM www.rmauctions.com
Shannons www.shannons.com.au
Silver www.silverauctions.com

11 Paperwork
– correct documentation is essential!

The paper trail

Classic, collector and prestige vehicles usually come with a large portfolio of paperwork accumulated and passed on by a succession of proud owners. This documentation represents the real history of the car, and from it can be deduced the level of care the vehicle has received, how much it's been used, which specialists have worked on it, and the dates of major repairs and restorations. All of this information will be priceless to you as the new owner, so be very wary of cars with little or no paperwork to support their claimed history.

Registration documents

All countries/states have some form of registration for private vehicles whether its like the American 'pink slip' system or the British 'log book' system.

It is essential to check that the registration document is genuine, that it relates to the car in question, and that all the vehicle's details are correctly recorded, including chassis/VIN and engine numbers (if these are shown). If you are buying from the previous owner, his or her name and address will be recorded in the document: this will not be the case if you are buying from a dealer.

In the UK the current (Euro-aligned) registration document is named 'V5C,' and is printed in coloured sections of blue, green and pink. The blue section relates to the car specification, the green section has details of the new owner and the pink section is sent to the DVLA in the UK when the car is sold. A small section in yellow deals with selling the car within the motor trade.

Previous ownership records

Due to the introduction of important new legislation on data protection, it is no longer possible to acquire, from the British DVLA, a list of previous owners of a car you own, or are intending to purchase. This scenario will also apply to dealerships and other specialists, from who you may wish to make contact and acquire information on previous ownership and work carried out.

If the car has a foreign registration, there may be expensive and time-consuming formalities to complete. Do you really want the hassle?

Roadworthiness certificate

Most country/state administrations require that vehicles are regularly tested to prove that they are safe to use on the public highway and do not produce excessive emissions. In the UK that test (the 'MOT') is carried out at approved testing stations, for a fee. In the USA the requirement varies, but most states insist on an emissions test every two years as a minimum, while the police are charged with pulling over unsafe-looking vehicles.

In the UK the test is required on an annual basis once a vehicle becomes three years old. Of particular relevance for older cars is that the certificate issued includes the mileage reading recorded at the test date and, therefore, becomes an independent record of that car's history. Ask the seller if previous certificates are available. Without an MOT the vehicle should be trailered to its new home, unless you insist that a valid MOT is part of the deal. (Not such a bad idea this, as at least you will know the car was roadworthy on the day it was tested and you don't need to wait for the old certificate to expire before having the test done.)

In the UK, vehicles over 40 years old on May 20th each year, are exempt from MOT testing. Owners can still have the test carried out if they so wish.

Road licence

The administration of every country/state charges some kind of tax for the use of its road system, the actual form of the 'road licence' and, how it is displayed, varying enormously country to country and state to state.

Whatever the form of the road licence, it must relate to the vehicle carrying it and must be present and valid if the car is to be driven on the public highway legally.

Changed legislation in the UK means that the seller of a car must surrender any existing road fund licence, and it is the responsibility of the new owner to re-tax the vehicle at the time of purchase and before the car can be driven on the road. It's therefore vital to see the Vehicle Registration Certificate (V5C) at the time of purchase, and to have access to the New Keeper Supplement (V5C/2), allowing the buyer to obtain road tax immediately.

In the UK, classic vehicles 40 years old or more on the 1st January each year get free road tax. It is still necessary to renew the tax status every year, even if there is no change.

If the car is untaxed because it has not been used for a period of time, the owner has to inform the licensing authorities.

Certificates of authenticity

It's possible to get a certificate proving the age and authenticity (eg engine and chassis numbers, paint colour and trim) of a particular vehicle. These are called Heritage Certificates, and if the vehicle comes with one of these it's a definite bonus. If you want to obtain such a certificate, go to www.heritage-motor-centre.co.uk.

If the vehicle has been used in European classic car rallies, it may have a FIVA (Federation Internationale des Vehicules Anciens) certificate. The so-called 'FIVA Passport,' or 'FIVA Vehicle Identity Card,' enables organisers and participants to recognise whether or not a particular vehicle is suitable for individual events. If you want to obtain such a certificate go to www.fbhvc.co.uk or www.fiva.org, there will be similar organisations in other countries, too.

Valuation certificate

Hopefully, the vendor will have a recent valuation certificate, or letter signed by a recognised expert stating how much he, or she, believes the particular vehicle to be worth (such documents, together with photos, are usually needed to get 'agreed value' insurance). Generally such documents should act only as confirmation of your own assessment of the vehicle rather than a guarantee of value, as the expert has probably not seen the vehicle in the flesh. The easiest way to find out how to obtain a formal valuation is to contact the owners' club.

Service history

Often these vehicles will have been serviced at home by enthusiastic (and hopefully capable) owners for a good number of years. Nevertheless, try to obtain as much service history and other paperwork pertaining to the vehicle as you can. Naturally, dealer stamps, or specialist garage receipts score most points in the value stakes.

However, anything helps in the great authenticity game, items like the original bill of sale, handbook, parts invoices and repair bills, adding to the story and the character of the vehicle. Even a brochure correct to the year of the vehicle's manufacture is a useful document and something that you could well have to search hard to locate in future years. If the seller claims that the vehicle has been restored, expect receipts and other evidence from a specialist restorer.

If the seller claims to have carried out regular servicing, ask what work was completed, when, and seek some evidence of it having been carried out. Your assessment of the vehicle's overall condition should tell you whether the seller's claims are genuine.

Restoration photographs

If the seller tells you that the vehicle has been restored, then expect to be shown a series of photographs taken while the restoration was under way. Pictures taken at various stages, and from various angles, should help you gauge the thoroughness of the work. If you buy the vehicle, ask if you can have all the photographs, as they form an important part of its history. It's surprising how many sellers are happy to part with their car and accept your cash, but want to hang on to their photographs! In the latter event, you may be able to persuade the vendor to get a set of copies made.

12 What's it worth?
– let your head rule your heart

Condition

If the vehicle you've been looking at is really bad, you've probably not bothered to use the marking system in Chapter 9 – 60 minute evaluation. You may not have even got as far as using that chapter at all!

If you did use the marking system in Chapter 9, you'll know whether the vehicle is in Excellent (maybe concours), Good, Average or Poor condition or, perhaps, somewhere in-between these categories.

Land Rover magazines run a regular price guide. If you haven't bought the latest editions, do so now and compare their suggested values for the model you are thinking of buying. Also look at the auction prices they're reporting. Values have been fairly stable for some time, but some models will always be more sought-after than others. Trends can change, too. The values published tend to vary from one magazine to another, as do their scales of condition, so read carefully the guidance notes they provide. Bear in mind, a vehicle that is truly a recent show winner could be worth more than the highest scale published. Assuming that the vehicle you are considering is not in show/concours condition, relate the level of condition that you judge it to be in with the appropriate guide price. How does the figure compare with the asking price? Before you start haggling with the seller, consider what affect any variation from standard specification might have on the vehicle's value.

If you are buying from a dealer, remember there will be a dealer's premium on the price.

Desirable options/extras

For collectors concerned with having the vehicle closely resemble its condition as it left the assembly line, factory-fitted desirable options included: a mechanical capstan winch or hydraulic drum winch, a front or central power take-off unit, towing equipment, and oil cooler – these are most of the main assembly line optional extras available for the early Series I onwards. A wide variety of other factory-fitted options became available in the ensuing years for Land Rovers covered by this guide. Collectors may need to establish whether any of these later options were available at the time of manufacture for a specific vehicle. Such later options could include: swivel hub gaitors, freewheeling hubs, Fairey overdrive, heavy-duty suspension, steering damper, split rim wheels, alternator, folding steps, mudflaps, windscreen washers, and a heater/demister.

For non-collectors, whose interests may be more focussed upon the suitability of the vehicle to match their requirements, options include: electric winch, rock sliders, underbody protection plates, parabolic springs, chequer-plate body panels, electronic ignition, additional lighting, alloy wheels, LPG conversion, weber carburettor, electric fan, a raised air intake, and a more powerful engine. Personal preferences vary enormously, however, so a non-collector may not regard all of the above options/extras as desirable.

Undesirable features

Any body part which introduces a visible hybrid characteristic to the vehicle, such as a Series III hinges on a Series II or IIA, or a Series II door on a Series I.

Headlights were moved out to the wings for the last two years of Series IIA production. The internally-mounted headlights are more iconic, and widely regarded as symbolic of a Series I, II or IIA Land Rover. Headlights in the wings tend to be regarded as indicative of a Series III.

Striking a deal

Negotiate on the basis of your condition assessment, mileage, and fault rectification cost. Also take into account the vehicle's specification. Be realistic about the value, but don't be completely intractable: a small compromise on the part of the vendor or buyer will often facilitate a deal at little real cost.

13 Do you really want to restore?
– it'll take longer and cost more than you think

Define 'restore'
Do you want to restore a vehicle to roadworthy condition, or do you want to return it to how it may have appeared just after leaving the factory? It took me 6 months to restore my Series IIA sufficiently to get it through its roadworthiness test – it had simply stood idle and unattended on grass for several years.

Practicality
A Series Land Rover was designed for ease of repair. Many mechanical parts are serviceable, and appropriate repair kits are available, as opposed to requiring off-the-shelf replacements.

Time allocation
It will take you longer than you think. Having both a full-time job and a Land Rover restoration leaves little time for anything else. Decide whether you should work on those aspects that will allow you to get it to a roadworthy state first, or jump in at the deep end and commit to a plan that leaves the vehicle unusable until project completion. If you are hoping to work over a winter period, less daylight hours requires adequate indoor lighting and heating.

Immobilised by a seized engine, and too tall to fit in the garage. Each restoration project comes with its own challenges.

Restoration can be planned such that the vehicle looks complete and is roadworthy, but some repairs remain to be done at your leisure. A running restoration.

Economics
Restoration is not economical, even if you do all the labour yourself.
Expect professional restoration costs to greatly exceed the cost of the vehicle. You will not recover your investment, no matter how concours the restoration is; but what price can you put on achievement?

Space
Restoration requires lots of it; preferably indoors, otherwise you'll be weather-dependent. Do you have this space available yourself or courtesy of a friend, or could you rent it economically? When compelled to work outdoors with limited hard standing, I have found a large sheet of 10mm plywood useful as a base for the lifting crane when removing the engine or gearbox: the width of the plywood is dictated by the distance between the front wheels, then at least some work can be done indoors.

The best source of used parts in the UK are the various Land Rover shows that run from May to September.

Logistics
Can you realistically source all the parts required, in the order needed, as financing allows and according to the projected schedule? If you are held back whilst waiting for parts, your schedule crumbles. You may need to pay more for parts to get them quickly, rather than wait for the free postage option from some suppliers.

Human resources
'More hands make light work,' so is there any help available? Keep in mind that potentially inconvenienced family members and neighbours need to be supportive of your endeavours.

Tools/equipment
A variety of specialist tools, such as a torque wrench and engine hoist, will be required. If you don't already have these, and can't borrow them as required, you need to budget for purchase or hire them. If restoration involves welding, do you have the equipment and the skill required?

14 Paint problems
– bad complexion, including dimples, pimples and bubbles

Paint faults generally occur due to lack of protection and/or maintenance, or to poor preparation prior to a repaint or touch-up. Some of the following conditions may be present in the vehicle you're looking at.

Orange peel
This appears as an uneven paint surface, similar to the appearance of the skin of an orange. The fault is caused by the failure of atomized paint droplets to flow into each other when they hit the surface. It's sometimes possible to rub out the effect with proprietary paint cutting/rubbing compound, or very fine grades of abrasive paper. A respray may be necessary in severe cases. Consult a bodywork repairer/paint shop for advice.

Cracking
Severe cases are likely to have been caused by too heavy an application of paint (or filler beneath the paint). Also, insufficient stirring of the paint before application can lead to the components being improperly mixed, and cracking can result. Incompatibility with the paint already on the panel can have a similar effect. To rectify it's necessary to rub down to a smooth, sound finish before respraying the problem area.

Crazing
Sometimes the paint takes on a crazed rather than a cracked appearance when the problems mentioned under 'Cracking' are present. This problem can also be caused by a reaction between the underlying surface and the paint. Paint removal and respraying the problem area is usually the only solution.

Blistering
Almost always caused by corrosion of the metal beneath the paint. Perforation will usually be found in the metal, and the damage will be worse than that suggested by the area of blistering. The metal will have to be repaired before repainting.

Micro blistering
Usually the result of an economy respray where inadequate heating has allowed moisture to settle on the vehicle before spraying. Consult a paint specialist, but damaged paint will have to be removed before partial or full respraying. Can also be caused by car covers that don't 'breathe.'

Fading
Some colours, especially solid reds, are prone to fading

f subject to strong sunlight for long periods without polish protection. Sometimes proprietary paint restorers and/or paint cutting/rubbing compounds will retrieve the situation. Often a respray is the only real solution.

Peeling

Often a problem with metallic paintwork starts when the sealing lacquer becomes damaged and begins to peel off. Poorly applied paint may also peel. The remedy is to strip and start again!

Dimples

Dimples in the paintwork are caused by the residue of polish (particularly silicone types) not being removed properly before respraying. Paint removal and repainting is the only solution.

Dents

Small dents are usually easily cured by the 'Dentmaster,' or equivalent process, that sucks or pushes out the dent (as long as the paint surface is still intact). Companies offering dent removal services usually come to your home: consult your telephone directory.

15 Problems due to lack of use

– just like their owners, Land Rovers need exercise!

Vehicles, like humans, are at their most efficient if they exercise regularly. A run of at least ten miles, once a week, is recommended, especially for Series Is.

Seized components
• Pistons in brake/clutch, slave and master cylinders can seize
• The clutch plate may bond to the flywheel and seize if left unused for months
• Handbrakes (parking brakes) can seize if the linkages rust
• Pistons can seize in the bores due to corrosion

Fluids
• Old, acidic, oil can corrode bearings
• Uninhibited coolant can corrode internal waterways
• Lack of antifreeze in cold climates can cause core plugs to be pushed out, or even crack the block or head
• Silt settling and solidifying can cause overheating
• Brake fluid absorbs water from the atmosphere, and should be renewed every two years
• Old fluid with a high water content can cause corrosion and pistons/callipers to seize (freeze), and also brake failure when the water turns to vapor near hot braking components

Marks on this clutch lining show it had bonded to the flywheel and would not release due to flywheel corrosion.

Tyre problems
• Tyres that have had the weight of the vehicle on them in a single position for some time will develop flat spots, resulting in some (sometimes temporary) vibration. The tyre walls may have cracks or bulges (blister-type), meaning new tyres are needed

Shock absorbers (dampers)
• With lack of use, the dampers lose their elasticity or even seize. Creaking, groaning and stiff suspension are signs of this problem

Rubber and plastic
• Radiator hoses may have perished and split, possibly resulting in the loss of all coolant

Modern fuel degrades over time. The tank can be emptied via the drain plug. Dispose of fuel in an environmentally friendly way.

The diaphragm on mechanical fuel pumps can harden and then tear. Overhaul kits are available.

Rubber seals will harden and leak in the brake and clutch master and slave cylinders. Replace all seals.

• Window and door seals can harden and leak
• Gaitors/boots can crack
• Wiper blades will harden
• The diaphragm in the distributor's vacuum advance can harden, resulting in retarded ignition timing. This leads to a hotter than normal engine, risk of burnt values, and a waste of fuel

Electrics
• The battery will be of little use if its not been charged for many months
• Earthing/grounding problems are common when the connections have corroded
• Old bullet and spade type electrical connectors commonly rust/corrode, and will need disconnecting, cleaning, and protection (eg Vaseline)
• Sparkplug electrodes will often have corroded in an unused engine
• Wiring insulation can harden and fail

Rotting exhaust system
• Exhaust gas has a high water content so exhaust systems corrode very quickly from the inside when the vehicle is not used

16 The Community

– key people, organisations and companies in the Land Rover world

Clubs

UK

Approximately 100 local and national Land Rover clubs. Details on the 'UK Clubs' page of www.series123.com

The Land Rover Register (1948-53)
http://www.lrr48-53.info

The Land Rover Series One Club Ltd
www.lrsoc.com

Land Rover Series I 107 Station Wagon Register
www.overscheenseweg7.nl/landrover_lr107sw/

Land Rover Series 2 Club
www.series2club.co.uk/

Europe & some parts of the world
Details on the 'Clubs and Parts Suppliers' page of www.lrfaq.org

Australia & New Zealand
Clubs throughout both countries
Details on the clubs page of www.series123.com/AUS/

USA & Canada
Clubs in at least 26 States and 5 Provinces.
Details on the clubs page of www.series123.com/USA/

Main spares suppliers
UK
John Craddock Ltd
North Street
Bridgtown
Cannock
Staffordshire
WS11 0AZ

Tel: + 44 (0)1543 577207
Fax: +44 (0) 1543 460160
Email: general@johncraddockltd.co.uk
Web: www.johncraddockltd.co.uk

Dunsfold DLR
Alfold Road
Dunsfold
Surrey
GU8 4NP
Tel: +44 (0) 1483 200567
Fax: +44 (0) 1483 200738
Email: dlr@dunsfold.com
Web: www.dunsfold.com

Pegasus Parts
Surrey
UK
Email: pegasusparts@btinternet.com
Web: www.pegasusparts.co.uk

USA
Rovers North Inc
1319 Vermont Route 128
Westford
VT USA 05494-9601
Tel: 1-802-879-0032
Web: www.roversnorth.com

British Pacific
26007 Huntington Lane
Unit 2
Valencia
California 91355
Tel: 1-800-554-4133
Email: brtipac@aol.com
Web: www.britishpacific.com

Canada
3 Brothers Classic Rovers
Tel: 519-302-3227
Email: Sales@3BrothersClassicRovers.com
Web: www.3brothersclassicrovers.com

Australia
British Off Road
Bruce Highway
Forest Glen
Sunshine Coast
Queensland
Tel: 61 7 5445 1094
Email: enquiries@britishoffroad.com
Web: www.britishoffroad.com/

Magazines & books

Classic Land Rover
Key Publishing Ltd
PO Box 300
Stamford
Lincolnshire
PE9 1NA
Web: www.classiclandrover.com

Land Rover Monthly
The Publishing House
2 Brickfields Business Park
Woolpit
Suffolk
IP30 9QS
Web: www.lrm.co.uk

Land Rover Owner International
Bauer
Media House
Lynchwood
Peterborough PE2 6EA
Web: www.lro.com

*Land Rover Series II, IIA and III
(Maintenance and Upgrades Manual)* by
Richard Hall. ISBN 1785001352

*Land Rover Story: 1948-71 (Brooklands
Road Tests)* by James Taylor.
ISBN 1855203391

*Practical Classics on Land Rover
Series 1 Restoration: The Complete
DIY Series 1 Land Rover Restoration
Guide (Practical Classics)* by Clarke R M
(Editor). ISBN 1855207583

*Land Rover Series I Workshop
Manual (Official Workshop Manuals)*
by Brooklands Books Ltd.
ISBN 0907073980

*Land Rover Series 1 Parts
Catalogues 1948-53 (Official Parts
Catalogue)* by Brooklands Books Ltd.
ISBN 1855201194

*Land Rover Series 1 Parts
Catalogues 1954-58 (Official Parts
Catalogue)* by Brooklands Books Ltd.
ISBN 1855201070

*Land Rover Series 2 and 2A, 1958-71
(Brooklands Road Tests)* by R M Clarke.
ISBN 0948207981

*Land Rover Diesel Series IIA and III
1958-85 Service and Repair Manual
(Haynes Service and Repair Manuals)*
by J H Haynes and John S Mead.
ISBN 1859601790

*Land Rover Series 2, 2A and 3
1958-85 Service and Repair Manual
(Haynes Service and Repair Manuals)*
by J H Haynes and Marcus Daniels.
ISBN 1859601472

*Land Rover Series 2 and Early 2A
Bonnet Control Parts Catalogues
(Official Parts Catalogue)* by Brooklands
Books Ltd. ISBN 1855202387

*Land Rover Series 2A Bonneted
Control Parts Catalogue (Official Parts
Catalogue)* by Brooklands Books Ltd.
ISBN 1855202751

17 Vital statistics
– essential data at your fingertips

Production history
Series I 1948 to 1958

1595cc engine used was derived from the Rover 60 saloon car.
Permanent four-wheel drive with free-wheel device until late 1950.
1997cc engine used from August 1951.
1997cc engine fitted with water channels between all cylinders in 1953 due to a overheating problem.
86in and 107in wheelbases introduced in 1953.
88in and 109in wheelbases introduced in 1956.
2052cc diesel engine introduced in 1957 (no diesels before this).
211,000 Series Is produced, and about 70 per cent exported.

Series II 1958 to 1961

1.5in wider track than the Series I, also new hinges, side skirts, indicators, and tail lights. Glass was used instead of perspex for windows.
109in Station Wagon launched before end of 1958 with a 2.25-litre engine (derived from the Rover 80).
250,000th Land Rover produced in November 1959.
110,000 Series IIs produced, and about 70 per cent exported.

Series IIA 1961 to 1971

Introduced in September 1961 with a 2.25-litre diesel engine.
500,000th Land Rover produced in April 1966.
In 1966, the 109in Station Wagon, with a high-performance Weslake-head six-cylinder engine, was introduced to North America.
2625cc six-cylinder petrol engine was an option in the 109in from 1967 (derived from the Rover 100).
Zenith carburettor replaces Solex, and negative earth electrics used in 1967.
Headlamps in wings available overseas from April 1968, and in UK from February 1969
400,000+ Series IIAs produced, and majority exported.

Load capacities

Model	Min unladen weight	Max allowable weight
80inch 1948-51	2594lb (1340kg)	-
80inch 1952-54	2604lb (1181kg)	-
86inch 1954-56	2702lb (1228kg)	-
107inch 1954-58	3056lb (1389kg)	4556lb (2071kg)
88inch 1956-58	2740lb (1243kg)	4190lb (1901kg)
109inch 1956-58	3080lb (1397kg)	5185lb (2352kg)
88inch 1958-61	2900lb (1315kg)	4453lb (2020kg)
109inch 1958-61	3294lb (1494kg)	5905lb (2678kg)
88inch 1961-71	2953lb (1339kg)	4453lb (2020kg)
109inch 1961-71	3301lb (1497kg)	5905lb (2678kg)
109inch (6-cyl)	3459lb (1569kg)	5905lb (2678kg)
109inch ('1 ton')	3886lb (1763kg)	6750lb (3062kg)

The 'payload' is the load (excluding the driver and 1 passenger) that the vehicle may reasonably be expected to carry comfortably cross-country. It's generally around 1000lb (460kg) throughout the model range, except for the 1500lb (680kg) of the 109in '1 ton.'

Fluid capacities

Engine size	1595cc	1997cc	2052cc	2286cc	2625cc
Radiator	9.7-litre	9.7-litre	9.7-litre	10.2-litre (pet) 9.9-litre (die)	11.3-litre
Engine sump (including filter)	6.2-litre	6.2-litre	7.3-litre	7.1-litre	7.3-litre
Gearbox	1.4-litre	1.4-litre	1.4-litre	1.4-litre	1.4-litre
Transfer box	2.5-litre	2.5-litre	2.5-litre	2.5-litre	2.5-litre

Swivel hubs: 0.6-litre.
Differential (by type): Rover 1.7-litre (front and rear); Env 1.4-litre (rear), 1.2-litre (front); Salisbury 2.5-litre (front and rear)

Fuel tanks
All fuel tank capacities (including both petrol and diesel) are 10-gal (45-litre), except for the 109in six-cylinder and 109in Station Wagon, which are 15-gal (68-litre).

Turning circle
80in   33ft (10.1m)
86in   37ft (11.3m)
88in   42ft (12.8m)
107in   48ft (14.6m)
109in   48ft (14.6m)
Larger tyres increase the turning circle.

Tyre sizes
80in, 86in and 88in use 6.00-16in, 6.50-16 or 7.00-16in.
109in use 7.50-16in.

Fuel consumption
80in   1595cc petrol   25mpg
86in   1997cc petrol   21mpg
88in   2052cc diesel   28mpg
88in   2286cc petrol   18mpg
88in   2286cc diesel   28mpg
107in   1997cc petrol   20mpg
109in   2286cc petrol   18mpg
109in   2286cc diesel   28mpg
109in   2625cc petrol   14mpg
Sustained urban use will lower these figures. Use of four-wheel drive dramatically reduces them.

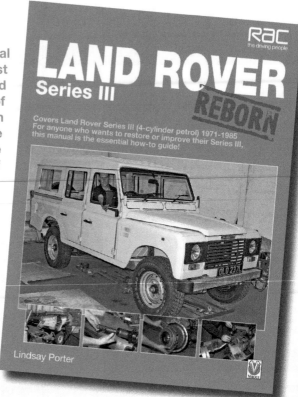

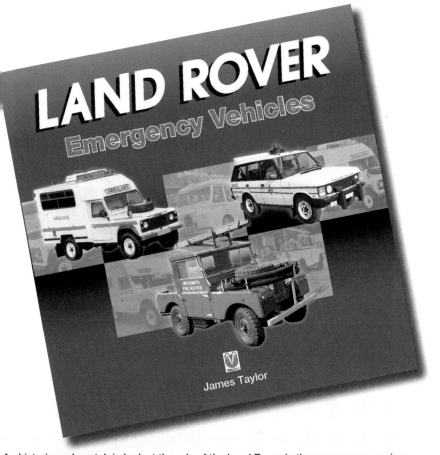

An historic and nostalgic look at the role of the Land Rover in the emergency services over the last 70 years. Land Rover products have been used by the emergency services almost from the moment the first model left the factory in 1948. The agility and size of these vehicles made them an immediate hit with fire services, where they initially became popular as factory fire tenders. Police forces were also attracted by the cross-country ability and versatility of Land Rovers, especially outside Britain, and, when long-wheelbase models provided extra space, they also became favourites for ambulance conversions.
This book will interest Land Rover enthusiasts and emergency-vehicle enthusiasts alike, with evocative photographs that illustrate both historic vehicles and more recent vehicles in action.

• Paper lined case • 25x25cm • 144 pages
• 367 colour pictures • ISBN: 978-1-787112-44-5

For more info on Veloce titles, visit our website at www.veloce.co.uk
• email: info@veloce.co.uk • Tel: +44(0)1305 260068

Index